THE WOMAN INSIDE OF ME

JAE ESCOTO

Published by Capturing Fire Press, Washington, DC

ISBN: 978-1-7328759-2-0

Capturing Fire Press is an independent publishing
house founded by Regie Cabico that seeks to
promote politically charged, performance &
experimental poetry of the highest quality by
diverse queer poets from around the globe.

Cover and book design by Sasha Sinclair/Studio
3440, Washington, DC

Printed in the United States of America

The voices in this book are representative of myself and the woman who lives inside of me (narrated in *italics*) as we journey through my transition from woman to man.

Written by Jae Escoto; Inspired by Jerrica Escoto.

For Noah, Jeremiah, and Greyson.

The Woman Inside of Me was first performed by Jae Escoto, directed by Regie Cabico with stage management provided by Sasha Sinclair as part of Capturing Fire Performance Festival, June 1, 2019.

Table of Contents

FOREWORD

Her name was Jerrica. She talked a lot of shit, wrote
poems about opening the same veins as me, questioned
grammar rules and laughed.... Loudly. When you call
someone your best friend, you form a bond that is so far
beyond romance and siblinghood; shit is magical.
Ducky, is my best-friend, Jerrica, will always have a
special place in my heart but Jae, a man I have come to
love... this space is for you. Thank you for getting all of
our inside jokes.

We work so hard to find ourselves.
We curl our tongues so tightly around monikers and
identity.
Watch as our names try to fit comfortably in people's
mouths.
Wrestle with the inability to try new things, to see things
differently...

The moments shared in these pages are not simply for
you to ease
Into Jae and figure out how to pluck the Jerrica from
your teeth.
This is for anyone who has the audacity to ask, "Why?"

This is for family
This is for all of the times Jerrica
Opened her chest so Jae could see who was looking in
This is about fruition and acceptance.
This is about a Son, ensuring his parents understand
He did not try to kill their daughter, only wanted to
Be their Sun.
This is the pain and labor
The mourning, ascension and rebirth.
A trifecta of being.

Jae, you will always be my Ducky. We will always look good together even though we are not together. Acceptance, is nothing you will have to ask for here. You will be the God-Father to my children – they will deserve an uncle who has mastered duality. Your story, is brilliant as are you.

"We write to taste life twice, in the moment and in retrospect" – Anaïs Nin

I love you, Forever. -Boop

A NOTE TO THE READER

At the time of publishing this book, I have been out as a trans man to a handful of close family and friends for 3 years, out to my work for 1 year, out to my entire family for 7 months, out to everyone on my social media for 1 month, and on hormone replacement therapy for 6 months. This book is a chronology of my transition journey from pre-testosterone, leading up to the decision of taking testosterone, then starting testosterone. This book is also a chronology of my relationship with my trans identity for the past 3 years.

My transition isn't a straight, linear narrative (and I would argue most aren't). The excerpts in this book are a true reflection of what it has looked like for me to honor all of my parts, all of my versions, all of me. If during some parts of this book I sound messy...that's because at this current stage of my transition, I *am* messy.

My emotions are all over the place. My wants, needs, and desires change daily, sometimes by the hour, and even by the minute. I am slowly coming into myself as a man and figuring out what that means for me—and for me, only.

My transition has also been a true spiritual passage. The Woman in this book is much bigger than gender. I came into my spirituality looking toward and seeking guidance in the form of a Woman—of the Feminine—and I only know spirituality through that Woman. I don't know my spirituality in the form of a Man, except to say I know I am piloted by both the Feminine and the Masculine (as energies). But to preserve my spirituality is also to preserve the Woman inside me, the Woman outside of me, and the Woman all around me. She is the voice of compassion, empathy, and as one of my angels have called it: liquid love.

With that said, I would be remiss to not communicate with you that this book is MY trans narrative and is by no means indicative of other trans stories and experiences. Just like how all trans bodies do not look the same, our stories don't, either.
My hope for this book is to disrupt the conversation around what it means to have a trans identity. I don't believe that our thinking around transness has to be so binary and divided into strict understandings of gender, that male and female are mutually exclusive. The way we understand what it means to be trans can, instead, be celebrated in the same expansive and liberating way that we must learn to love ourselves when life calls for it. While I am a trans man, I am not me without also acknowledging the woman I came from.

I want this book to make a space for new dialogue around transitions and evolve out of the understanding that gender and gender expression is an entire spectrum. And where we fall on that spectrum is completely contingent upon where we WANT to fall on it at any day, at any time.

My story is vulnerable and raw. The excerpts in this book have come from the deepest parts of me that I have not allowed anyone to come close to. Because of this, I am inherently protective of my story. How I talk about my transition, my body, my family, my lovers, to publish these stories is to publish what I keep most in the dark. Ultimately, just as much as I had to step out of the darkness and into the light, so did my story.

This book is not a way for me to coddle the reader's experience of how to actively listen to a trans narrative.

This book, instead, is a way for me to promote reciprocity in healing from both writer to reader and to embrace my messiness. To own up to my messiness, to be proud of it, and to share with the world what one person's story looks like when you finally declare...

This is me.

ACKNOWLEDGMENTS

I am full of overwhelm and gratitude as I think of all those who have stood by my side throughout this journey.

First and foremost, to the Moon and my angels for your light, guidance, and for the humbling joy it has been for me to surrender, to fiercely believe, in something much bigger than me – much bigger than all of this. I could not have started this transition without your divinity, encouragement, and love.

To my parents, Emerito and Bernadette Escoto, for showing me unconditional love and true compassion. It is your model of love that has taught me what genuine kindness towards myself could look and feel like. I am one of the lucky ones to have parents who encourage their children to do whatever it takes to be happy. I love you both – more than words can say. Everything I do is always to make you two proud.

To my best friends and siblings:

Maricon, my Reject. I am convinced that you naming me is what catapulted the creation of this bond that is so special to me. You've been my rock, my voice of reason (even though I never listen), and where I have gone to fall apart knowing very well your love would bring me back together. I love you so much.

Bianca, I call you my little big sister because I am so protective of you and your good heart. I am proud to call myself your sibling. Some of the strength I've needed to pull from others during my transition has come from witnessing you take on this world with so much care and empathy. I love you – especially for the times you have reminded me that life can truly be as simple as choosing to be happy.

Sean, the water that keeps my fire balanced. You show me every day that life doesn't always have to be taken so seriously. Some days, it has been your motivation that has gotten me out of bed and outside of my home to remind me that I can love who I am, be proud of who I am, at whatever stage I am in. I can't count the times I was in the dark and you pulled me back into the light. I love you, little bro.

To the extended Escoto and Carpio family for your unwavering love and support. I thank you and I am beyond lucky to come from so much love and beauty.

Grandma Ising – there has never been a time, both while you were still here with us and after your passing, that you never came through for me if I asked for anything: a quarter for the ice cream man, more rice, or help looking for spiritual answers. I feel you all around me constantly. It was your fierce belief in God that inspired me to look for my own refuge. I love you. Thank you.

My protectors from the night: I didn't know if I could do this transition without you. I will always call for you and look for you in every corner I turn, in every new person I meet, in any new connection I make. You three are a story I am too stubborn to stop telling. And I miss you so much. Cap – for the stories outside of these three that will remain with us, that will keep us close, inside of your fire, and inside of my light.

Freda Salamy – my most expensive friend, a healer, a coach, a kindred spirit whose grace has provided a space where I have felt the most safe, the most seen, the most me. I am truly grateful for this lifetime together and for your invaluable insight that has undoubtedly saved my life.

Thank you to Chelsea Cormier for a friendship I truly treasure and for the time you spent giving me feedback through the phases of this book. My gratitude to all of my friends back home in San Diego, the Curriculum & Learning team – especially Kelly Garland, to those I have given parts of my past self to as I step into the future, for those who have loved me wholly throughout all of my messiness, the ones who have thought to ask permission, first, before any touch, to those whose thick skin never got cut from my sometimes jagged edges, especially Rachel Wallis, thank you.

To the readers of this book and some of my greatest friends: Catherine "Dr. C" Cucinella, Regie Cabico, and Matt Storm - for believing in this book but more importantly, always believing in me. Sasha Sinclair for your collaboration with the book cover and for how effortlessly you manage everything. Thank you.

Tabitha Brown, my Boopster, for writing the foreword of this book and being my we-look-cute-together-but-we-ain't-together best friend. I am so lucky the world brought us together in San Diego and then had us follow each other to the east coast. Always your Ducky. Together forever. I love you.

Sanam, all of this started with you. Thank you for the day you called me man for the first time, before anyone else, before even I could. There was a great sacrifice we both made to find ourselves here: apart but together all the same. When life finally takes us on our own paths without each other, I will find peace and gratitude knowing I was loved by you.

Finally, to my nephews Noah, Jeremiah, and Greyson, the ones I have dedicated this book to. I love you three with a ferocity that even I couldn't have imagined was possible. When each of you were born, the ugly of this world slowly began to diminish more and more with every laugh, every dance, every kiss and hug you've given me, every moment I've held you all close. You three are reminders that there is, indeed, so much joy left for me to experience in my day to day. And I will fight to create a world for you just as beautiful as you have turned mine into.

"And the day came when the risk to remain tight in a bud was more painful than the risk it took to blossom."
- Anaïs Nin

THE WOMAN INSIDE OF ME

JAE ESCOTO

PROLOGUE

My father called me the other day. He had just gotten back from visiting my sister, her fiancé, and my new nephew in Hawaii. I asked how the visit went.

He sighed.

My father's sigh is the prerequisite to my response: "What happened?"

"Is your sister happy?"

My sister is 7 years older than me.

The story goes that the day I was born and I came out as another girl instead of the first boy, my mother cried and they didn't know what to name me. My sister stepped up after watching her favorite cartoon, Jem and the Holograms, and said, "We should name her Jerrica."

Being named after a cis white girl who leads a rock band is super problematic for me. But nevertheless, I think my sister naming me created the bond we have now. And I don't intend to legally change my name because of it.

My response to my father was:
"I don't think it's my place to say whether she's happy or not."

He began to cry on the phone. He told me he's worried about her because these days, she just doesn't seem to be the daughter he knows her to be.

"You know your sister. She's strong. I just want her to be happy."

If the day I tell my parents there was a mistake. And I actually came out as their first boy instead of their third girl…

Will my mother still cry?

Will they still not know how to name me?

Will my father call my sister and say, "Is Jae happy?"

Will he sob on the phone the same way he did with me?

Will he tell her he's worried about me?

Or will he tell her that these days, I don't seem to be the daughter he knows me to be.

Will my sister respond with, "Ask him if he is happy. It is not my place to say."

Will my pronoun roll off her tongue with the same confidence she had the same day she chose my name?

In a Filipino family where I am both the rock and the hard place, people wonder why it would be difficult to come out if I already did for being gay.

The night I came out to my father, his silence for the next few years drowned out the sound of self-love knocking down my door.

To tell my father that the closet is still in his home

In my childhood bedroom

Creaking to match the sound in my gut

My stomach

A dusty journal with all of my secrets

And I am one cough away from saying to my father,

"I am still strong.
I am strong because I come from a lineage of brown
people who had no other choice but to be strong in
order to survive.
I have no other choice but to be strong
In order to survive inside of a body that does not feel
like my own."
And I am here.
This is me.
Will you still love me?
Will you cry to me and tell me you want me to be
happy?

Will you say,
I'm not the daughter you know me to be...
I'm not the daughter...

I'm the son.

THE WOMAN INSIDE OF ME – A
BEGINNING

Some nights,
I wake up choking to the woman inside of me
Trying to claw her way out of my mouth
She waits until I am sleeping
Because it is the only time I do not try to forget her

Sometimes,
When I am alone
I can hear her weeping in between the times I inhale
And exhale
When I bind my chest
I feel more than just the suffocation of my body
I feel her inside of me gasping for air
I know she is terrified that
I am trying to squeeze her out of me for good

For a while, I tried.
I swallowed her in front of other men to not seem weak
I hardened any time I felt her welling up behind my eyes
Used her as a scapegoat whenever anger was the only
prayer in my mouth
Blamed her for the depression
The anxiety
The dysmorphia and dysphoria
The dirty looks in public restrooms and fitting rooms
For being a god damn box to check on paperwork
I hated her for having the audacity to stay even after I
demanded her to leave

I also mourned
And I grieved
I didn't know how to say goodbye
I didn't know if I had to

When my therapist said I have internalized misogyny
I cried until the woman in me finally poured out of my
eyes
And onto the floor
She has never said, "I told you so"
She has only ever offered me a book of poems written
by a person I used to be
And now,
Here
In front of this mirror that I beg to tell me lies
I am trying to find a voice that resembles something
familiar
But I've only ever performed my poems in a higher
pitch
And I fear a lower frequency will mean I will relearn
how to be quiet

When all I want to do is scream
I am here
This is me

But my refusal to remember her
Is also my refusal to become a man who is not victim to
fragile masculinity

To be a man
Does not mean to forget all the parts of me that
is woman
That is soft
That is compassionate
That is empathetic
That is the only version of myself I have ever been
damn proud of to become

The day
That I can embrace my femininity
Will be the day I have stepped into my true masculinity

I would be lying
If I were to say the noise of patriarchy does not
keep me up at night

Sometimes,
I let her out before I go to bed
We do not speak
I do not remember the last time I looked her in the eye
But she just lies next to me
Silent

She puts her arms around me to remind me I am not
alone
And sometimes,
It is the only way I can be put to sleep

To dismiss her
Is to dismiss the fact that she is the reason why I am still
alive
I am nothing
Without all the different parts I have been and will
become

I am nothing
Without the woman who lives inside of me.

ON DUALITY

Here, I am set ablaze
My skeleton – a mere reflex, waiting for you t(w)o
Touch me in the parts I cannot control
I have watched my body move in a way that is unfamiliar
It is dangerous; but the thrill is a backbone
And this is the first I am experiencing what it is to be
alive
Human, lover, all the man in me, all the woman left
behind

There, you will find me soft
A gentle that blooms in Wintertime
My courage surpasses gender inside these walls
To love there is to love ferociously
The hardest of choices, the easiest of futures
Still human, still lover, still all this man in me
But a woman left behind.

JANUARY 27, 2017

I just realized that the only time I have ever received love or attention were the times I was softer. More passive. More woman. The last time my mother called me pretty was around 2013. It was post-surgery – so I was at my skinniest. I wore tighter clothes. My hair was curly, longer, more feminine.

The last time a man hit on me, it was 2012. I think he liked my poetry more than me but he called me beautiful.

The last time I slept with a man, he commented on how beautiful my breasts were.

I got more attention and love. I was attractive.

Last month, my mother was looking at a photo of our family and said to my brother, "You look handsome here." I waited. I wanted her to tell me I looked handsome, too. I wanted her to notice that I wasn't getting fatter. My back, arms, and chest are getting wider because of muscle I have been trying so hard to build. I wanted her to see the muscle was helping my posture. I wanted her to see I walk a little taller, now.

She never said anything. I cried.

How do you start to love the body you're in when the ones you love don't know how to love it, first?

SHE WINS THE WAR

I'm still here.

I fashion a white cotton boxer brief
Into a white flag
But she reminds me of the blood
I try to wash it way
It keeps coming

She keeps coming.

OH, SORRY

My voice is a boom box without batteries
I raise it in the air
Hoping the whistle of the wind fashions me a tone
Much more baritone than this

The public restrooms are dirty closets I thought I
already came out of
But they are more for the courage of coming in
Into so much light that it actually feels as blinding as the
dark

I'm in the men's clothing section at Nordstrom Rack
But I walk into the women's fitting room for safety
I am greeted by a woman who says, "You can't be here.
The men's fitting room is downstairs."
"I know that," I say.
She says, "Oh, sorry" and gives me a number

I want to say,
"Oh, sorry, you're right I will go downstairs. Thank you
for seeing me."
But I don't know if it's safer to stay here
Or to go there

I hurry as I undress
The stress of being found out
Or not at all
The layers feel like lies

I look in the mirror
Sir
I mean ma'am
I mean sir
Which one is it?
Which one is it.

IN THE DARK

Get up.

She draws the curtains and the sunlight beams at me.

"CLOSE THEM!" I yell as I take the pillow and bury my head under it. "It's too bright. I liked how dark it was in here."

You need to get your ass up. You have been in bed for days. I barely see you get up to pee.

"Leave me alone."

No.

"Leave me ALONE" I throw the pillow across the room and it hits her chest, then falls to the ground.

Yeah, because being left alone is what you ACTUALLY want, right? Like I didn't always want to be alone? Like I don't know what it's like for loneliness to drown you from the inside out? So much so that everything around you seems like it's under water? Sound seems muddled. Everything is a blur. You feel like you're suffocating. You think I don't know what it's like to ask for a savior? A life jacket? Someone to lean on who can swim us safely above water? You don't want to be left alone, Jae. You want someone here with you. You want someone to crawl in bed next to you and hold you and not say a thing but say everything all at once in the way they touch you. You want tenderness. You want someone who feels like the shoreline. And when your body breaks. When the water and the salt and the grief finally pours out of your eyes. You want someone who is a strong swimmer. Someone willing to start drowning in you only to finally meet you where it is familiar: in the blurry, muddled world around you. The world that does not make room for you. Does not understand you. The world

*that is waiting for you to finally choke on your vulnerabilities
enough to stop breathing completely.*

*You think I don't know what it's like to start thinking about my
breath differently? You think I don't know what any of this is
like?*

"Leave me alone," I say in a hesitant whisper.

She draws the curtains closed. She walks over to the bed
and slips inside the blanket with me. She holds me from
behind and strokes my hair.

I begin to cry.

*We have never been strong swimmers, my love. But we have always
survived the unapologetic sea. And if it is just us together on an
abandoned boat. If it is just the two of us in the middle of a body
of water that feels like your own body. A body that feels like you
will never find your way home...*

There will still be us.

And as for this entire world that doesn't see you? Well...

They could never love you like I love you, anyway.

TOP SURGERY

If I slice around the mountain
And reshape you into flatlands
Will I plateau?
Or become a scenic route?
A spectacle?
A gaze?
Will my eyes become a moat?
Will my chest resemble a tundra of stunted growth?
Will my scars bend like the Ganges?
Only to ash into who I was
Then resurrect into something more holy
More sacred
Than all this flesh.

WHEN WE BOTH BLEED

She slams the door and I hear her stomping up the stairs.

I sigh.

"It's nothing personal!" I yell.

More stomps. Then glass shattering.

I jolt up and run upstairs. She's crying on the bathroom floor and picking up large shards of glass with her fingers. The vanity mirror is broken.

I rush over. "Don't touch it! You'll cut yourself," I say. "Back up."

She pauses and looks up at me, glass still in her hands.

Oh, I can't have cuts but you are in complete right to cut off my breasts? And for what? What's wrong with the sports bras? And the tape? They've been working just fine.

"They DON'T work just fine. The sports bras kill my back and shoulders. The tape chafes my skin. You complain when I use a binder—"

BECAUSE I SUFFOCATE WHEN YOU WEAR IT!

She screams as she throws the glass towards me.

I duck but one of the shards hits my cheek and I start to bleed. She gasps then immediately runs over, holds my face in her hands, and wipes the blood from my face with her fingers. She is still crying, but her sobs are softer. They're more gentle—she is more gentle. She opens a drawer and grabs a cotton ball and rubbing alcohol. Before she puts it to my face, I grab her wrist.

"Just stop," I plea.

She stops crying and looks at me. I can feel the blood dripping down my cheek and a drop falls to my chest. She puts her palm on the part of my chest where the blood has stained my shirt. Some of our blood smears on to her hand.

What if this is the start of you wanting to remove all of me?

She wipes the remaining tears on her face with her palm that has our blood on it. She looks at us in the vanity mirror. The shattered glass is posing an illusion that we are apart even while standing right next to each other.

Do you see? We've already begun to separate.

LOST

I woke up this morning and she was not next to me.
I don't know where she is.

I don't know who I am.

THIS ONE LAST TIME

*You have to let me see them one last time before you go on
testosterone. PLEASE. You never do anything for me. All you
do is take and take and take from ME. What am I? What have
I ever been except a woman trying to figure out my worth? You're
doing that thing again...that thing where you're being impulsive
and you just want things fast and right NOW but you KNOW
WHAT. You need to just fucking slow down, okay?! Just slow
the fuck down. I need to see mom and dad one last time before I
start to disappear from them. I need to see our siblings. Our
nephews—god, our sweet sweet nephews. They have to see their
auntie. They have to know that I am here. They have to know
that I will always be here. You can't just DO this. You can't just
send a letter to mom and dad and then immediately start taking
injections. It's been ONE WEEK since you've talked to the
doctor. ONE WEEK. WHY can't you wait another month?
Another two months? Why can't you wait until early next year
when our older sister visits San Diego and the entire family will be
together again? When was the last time the entire family was
together like that?? WHEN? I DON'T EVEN
REMEMBER WHEN. I DON'T REMEMBER MOST
THINGS ANYMORE BECAUSE YOU ARE
MAKING ME FORGET. I WANT TO SEE MOM
AND DAD. I WANT TO HUG MOM AND DAD. I
WANT TO PLAY GAMES WITH THE BOYS AND I
WANT THEM TO KNOW THAT THEIR AUNTIE
IS RIGHT HERE. I AM RIGHT HERE, YOU SON
OF A BITCH. CAN'T YOU SEE. I AM RIGHT
FUCKING HERE. YOU HAVE TO LET ME SEE
THEM AGAIN. DON'T TAKE THEM AWAY
FROM ME SO SOON. Everyone already doesn't see me
anymore. They see you. You with your perfect haircut and your
clothes and your charm and the way you make them all laugh and
feel good. When was the last time you made ME feel good? Huh?
WHEN? If you stopped being such a selfish fucking bastard,
maybe you'd be able to pause and see that you're not the only one*

here. IT'S NOT JUST YOU. IT'S ME, TOO. I AM
HERE, TOO, JAE. YOU ARE HERE WITH ME. I
DESERVE—NO—I DEMAND THAT YOU LET
ME SEE THEM ONE LAST TI—

Okay.

What?

Okay. I said okay.

...okay.

QUIET

It's been quiet for the past few days. She went away after our last fight. I'm not sure if me telling her I would have her see our family one last time is what she actually wanted to hear. I'm not sure if that is actually what she's fighting for. I'm having a hard time getting her to understand that just because my physical form changes, it doesn't mean that she stops existing. She doesn't stop existing. I am not a man without her. I can't be a man without her—not a good one. Behind every good man is every single woman who has built that man. I was not brave enough to be a woman in this life. The strength and courage it takes for me to transition is nothing compared to the strength and courage it takes to be unapologetically woman.

I close my eyes to find her and she is not here. I'll keep waiting. She has to know that I don't want her to go away. I know it seemed that way before. But it's not true. I know she is hurting as I am here—a shadow man. Trying to find my soul. Trying to find my light. I look toward her for help because I see the Goddess in her. She has been a Queen. Her feet have been kissed. She has had loyal protectors bow and bend their knees. That woman that I experienced to be for just a few years—it still felt like it wasn't my destiny. Just hers. Her destiny in a different life than this one. A destiny much bigger than what is mundane. Much bigger than all of this humanity. I could only be in her way of true spiritual greatness. I am a man in the most human of form. But she. She is a woman that transcends flesh and bones. She transcends existence.

And I hope she comes back soon.

HER RETURN

You should tell them.

I turn around and she's standing at the doorway. Her hair is unbrushed and she looks like she hasn't slept for days.

"Where have you been?"

You should tell them.

She walks towards me and sits on my lap. She moves the hair out of my eyes and kisses me on the head.

Are you hurting today?

"Yes."

What's your pain-level?

"I don't know. A 7?"

I'm sorry I wasn't with you at the ER.

"That's okay. I know you had to go."

I realized something when I went away...

"Oh? What's that."

I'm in pain, too.

"I know you are—that's why I said we can go home one last time and—"

No. I mean…I'm in pain, too. With you. With your chronic migraines. And your chronic neck and back pain. How fatigue and weak you feel. I've felt that, too, all of this time with you.

"I'm sorry."

Don't be. I'm sorry nothing has ever helped us. We tried, though, didn't we? With the massage, the acupuncture, the craniosacral therapy (what even WAS that?), the chiropractor, the pills. We really tried.

"Yeah, we did."

We tried all but this one thing.

"What?"

Accepting ourselves.

She gets off my lap and moves towards the shower.

It's time to finally wash this all away, my love. We start anew today. Together.

She steps into the shower and begins to sing Hailee Steinfeld, "Love Myself."

I laugh.

Welcome home, my love.

THE MORNING I CAME OUT TO OUR PARENTS

"Hey. You up?"

Hey, you. Good morning. Why are you awake so early?

"Why are you awake so early?"

Um, you woke me up.

"Oh."

What's wrong, sweetheart?

"Nothing."

You didn't sleep, did you?

"No."

Alright, come here.

She outstretches her arms and gestures for me to lie on her chest.

"No, I don't feel like it."

It's going to be okay.

"I know."

Do you actually know that?

"No."

Well, I know. And it's going to be okay.

"Maybe I should wait."

Wait for what?

"I don't know. Maybe I should wait until I'm ready."

Ready for what?

"I don't know. Ready to tell them."

Are you actually not ready to tell them or are you scared?

I stay quiet.

They love you, you know.

"I know. I know we're lucky to have the parents we do. I know they try really hard to understand."

Remember when I came out to Dad?

"I don't know, sort of."

I basically pep-talked myself into finally treating him out to The Cheesecake Factory and trying to muster up the courage to blurt out, "Hey Dad, I'm gay!" in between bites of complimentary bread and sips of their sweet ass mango tea. But then appetizers came and went. Dinner came and went. Dessert even came and went and we know how overpriced that cheesecake is.

And then, remember? We went home. I sat in front of the TV with him, as I have done for so many years as a child the times I waited to muster up the courage to ask a question, and pretended to watch. Finally, I just blurted out, "Dad, I have a girlfriend." Then the silence. And more silence. And then, "Dad? Did you hear me?" Silence. Finally, he said, "What do you want me to do with that information?"

That was the most conversation we've had about identity but dad and mom have gotten better over the years. Am I right? They finally got on board with me getting married. They've made comments about accepting me. The point is, Jae, they try. They try with the best knowledge and resources they have as Filipino immigrants. I know, I get it. We always have to forgive. We have to lower our standards for understanding and compassion so that we don't continue to get hurt. I know that. But dad and mom love us in their own way. They might not accept the news right away— or at all—but they love us in their own way and the best way they know how. You have to trust that it's going to be okay.

"What if they start to love me differently? What if I stop being so close to mom and dad?"

Are you kidding me? GREAT. Then maybe they'll stop calling you every time they need something.

"C'mon."

Cool—ok. We aren't doing humor this morning. Sweetheart, will it be perfect? No. Will it take years for them to become comfortable with it? Yes. Will they ever get it right? I'm not sure. But here's what we do know. We know that we're hurting—physically, mentally, emotionally. We know that we have been hurting for as long as we can remember. I know you're terrified to make this step toward happiness. But this is who we are. We're bold. And we're driven and courageous and we are unapologetic of our opinions and desires because we know what we want and we don't rest until we have it.

"No, that's you."

No—that's US. The times you are most scared is when you forget that we are not separated. We are both man and woman and we swallow that entire spectrum whole. We are everything all at once happening at once.

I know you're scared. And that's okay. I want you to be scared. Because being scared means that you give a damn. But that fear doesn't have to be in front of you—it can be beside you. This is the only thing that we haven't tried. We've never tried asking mom and dad for help. We've never allowed ourselves to be vulnerable and to try and work collaboratively with the family when we are going through something. We haven't tried this one thing. And if it doesn't work, we will try it again for good measure. And maybe a third time. And then if we still feel this hopeless, we will find another option. We always find another option. It's just—it's time, Jae. You avoiding telling mom and dad does not make the truth untrue. Any time I have ever been scared, we have always done what we are afraid of, anyway. And we have always realized that the fear was always much bigger than we made it. Much much bigger.

"I'm still scared."

And that's okay.

"I'm ready now."

Ready for what.

I gesture to be held. She smiles.

Come here.

DEAR MOM AND DAD

I'm writing to you both to finally ask for help after trying to do things on my own for so many years. I finally hit my threshold with pain and suffering and I know that I need to start making changes in order to feel healthy. Being in constant emotional and physical pain is not something I want for my life anymore.

For years, I have repressed my identity and feelings toward my identity because I am terrified of disappointing you two. As I have gotten older and as my health has deteriorated more, I have realized that my fear of disappointing you two has made me sick. I have to come into my true self in order to feel happy and healthy again. That comes with the risk of hurting and disappointing you two. My hope is that you will love and accept me regardless of who I am.

This might not make a lot of sense to you both because of our generational difference but there is a term called "transgender." You might see this on TFC a lot with men who become women…but you don't really see it happen often for women who become men. These are people who truly feel like they are not their assigned gender at birth and they make changes to feel and see themselves as their true gender.

For the past few years, I have been seeing a therapist multiple times a month. As you know, since I've been 15, I was also on anti-depressants and I know that was also a scary time for you both since I was also hurting myself. The fact is that I have been extremely unhappy with myself for as long as I can remember. I try and stay strong for the family and for everyone around me but I think as I am getting older, it's getting harder for me to avoid my depression. It's getting harder for me to avoid some facts that I have learned about myself in these past few years: I am actually a transgender man and I feel like I am a man inside, and not a woman.

In DC and Maryland, I live a very different life compared to being at home in San Diego. At my work, I am acknowledged as transgender and my co-workers use he/him pronouns instead of she/her. When I do shows or conferences in DC, I am introduced as a transgender man.

Leaving San Diego gave me permission to finally explore my identity because I was too afraid to do so around family and friends that I have grown up with. I know you both keep asking why I just won't move back home and honestly, a big reason is because too much of my history is in San Diego. This is different than coming out as being gay – which I know was really hard for you both to accept already. There are real implications that can happen every day and I have tried and I've prayed to try and be "normal." I've asked God why I feel like this. Why I can't be happy as a girl and why so much inside of me feels like I am actually a boy.

As I've gone through therapy, I'm convinced that a lot of my health issues and chronic pain is caused by the fact that I don't recognize who I see in the mirror. And so I slowly started changing that – as you can see. I cut my hair really short. I started wearing men's clothes. When I visit home, I'm more comfortable wearing Dad's clothes vs. Mom's. I've just done a lot of small things these past few years so that I can feel more comfortable. But I'm finally ready for the next step. And this next step is the hardest and what I have avoided the most because I didn't want to disappoint you both.

I have decided that I want to start doing hormone therapy – this is where I would take injections of testosterone so that I can look more like a boy. I've spoken with multiple specialists about the best and safest way to go about this and I want you both to know that it is safe for me.

I will be the exact same person…except maybe I'll look a little more like Sean and maybe I will finally be happy and love myself. And maybe being able to be happy with myself will also cause me to be healthy again.

My concerns are that you will try and talk me out of this. My concerns are that you will think this is a phase or that you will think there is something wrong with me mentally. And I'm most of all concerned that you both will disown me.

There isn't anything wrong with me…except that maybe I was born in the wrong body. And my intention of this letter and finally coming out to you two is so that I can start asking for help because I need it. My role in the family has always been the strong rock for everyone. Because of this, I don't allow myself to be vulnerable or sensitive in front of everyone because I'm afraid of seeming weak. I don't want to lose the love and respect that I have received over the years. But I am making myself sick more and more as I avoid my truth. It's to the point where it has manifested in my body and I'm scared that if I don't start taking the right steps toward my happiness, then I will always be unhappy and always be in chronic pain.

Lately, you two have been telling me to not think so much. To stop stressing out. To let go of what I can't control. I think you two intuitively know there is something going on with me that is causing me to be this sick. No doctor or medication has been able to fix it for years. I've spent thousands of dollars trying to manage my pain and health but I know that once I can start accepting and loving myself...once I stop being afraid of disappointing you two...I can be healthy again.

I ask that you both help me on this journey. I'm not looking for you two to accept this right away or even accept it all if that is what you feel. I'm finally just asking for emotional help and support. I'm asking for you to love me despite the changes that might happen after I start hormone therapy. I'm asking for you to trust that I will always be the same Jerrica. I will always be the same caring and compassionate person you both raised me to be. I will always put my family first...but right now, I have to put myself first. And I pray that I will have your support.

Take your time letting this sink in and I'm ready to talk when you both are.

I love you,
J

WHEN MOM AND DAD SAID "WE LOVE YOU NO MATTER WHAT"

Tonight, the woman inside of me
And the emerging man
Became one whole.

Tonight, we are free for the first time in our lives.

MY LAST TRIP TO SAN DIEGO BEFORE STARTING TESTOSTERONE

I keep trying to reposition myself here as man. I touch
the walls of my childhood bedroom firmly. Imprinting
my found self into these walls. She recalls falling to her
knees one night in fierce prayer. There was a cross on
the wall; she doesn't remember how it got there. And
she didn't technically believe in any god at this point.
Went to church because our parents said so. But that's
about it. And so there she was. Both knees on the
ground and hands clasped in prayer. Any official prayer
escaping her and opened with tears as a SOS. "Let her
be okay. Let me save her." The woman inside of me
literally bursting at the seams, recollecting herself,
putting the stuffing back in that makes her body this
fucking soft, and she sews and sews and sews and it
bursts and she sews and sews. She took up knitting in
college, her roommate coming home every night to find
her on the couch knitting and knitting and wanting so
badly to put something together that started off as just a
line. Something linear. But here as she sews and knits,
what is linear expands outward until it is tentacles large
and moving and swaying and sometimes intertwining
but always coming from the same center.

When the woman inside of me is home on this trip—on
this final trip before I start testosterone—she
remembers these moments. As I go to work in my
parents' bedroom, she stays around the corner of the
hall in our bedroom. My parents' bedroom shares a wall
with ours. She remembers when we first moved into this
house in high school - she chose the room furthest from
our parents out of fury. Out of the need for space and
privacy. Instead, she chose the room closest to my
parents because of this very thin wall that heard the
phone calls at night and the depression back then. It was
so loud. And our parents, they didn't sleep that well, no

they didn't, especially the night when the blood that dropped from her wrist onto the carpet made a noise so loud my dad could have sworn it was a car crash right inside of his own home. But it was, wasn't it? The way she collided with herself?

She has me be the one to let this all out because she never could. Lovers would ask as they both lie naked smelling of sweat and hope, they would say, "Tell me something." And she would say, "Do you know what it is to be a woman? All of this woman I feel inside, it sometimes feels like she is a mutant. With abilities not fit for this Earth. Always a mystery. Feared of our potential. You ask me to tell you something and this is all I have. Tonight, I am the softest you will ever feel of me. Remember me this way."

She is acting like she didn't live in San Diego for nearly 27 years. I stepped into the shadows as I watched her take our nephew to the San Diego Zoo. "Those poor animals. I hope they're happy," she would think. At the zoo with her brother and cousin, they "she" her like it's not a mistake and she grows more and more into her light and turns back to look at me every now and then. I nod to her and she nods back and then she sees her friends who she has known for over 20 years. They are asking her questions about top surgery and hormone therapy and she turns and looks at me again and I nod to her and she says, "Let's see how it goes. Maybe I won't even like it. Maybe I'll just stay this way," and the subject is changed but it lingers in the room, I linger in the room, and now it is night time. I catch her in the bedroom crying on the floor staring at a framed photo of herself from the San Diego Union Tribune. I don't know what to say and so I don't show up to her entirely. She knows I am in the shadows watching silently. She stares again and again at her smile. Her ease. Her long hair. The eye liner. Then again at her smile.

It is no wonder she loves California so much. She shines so much brighter here.

AFTER PICKING UP PIZZA

It is the last night before flying back home to Maryland. I took my brother's car to pick up pizza for my extended family who were coming over to say goodbye. While I am in the car, I begin to cry. I take my hand and clutch on to my chest as if to hold her down from coming up for air. But it is too late. She's here and I am sobbing. We are both sobbing. I am pressing my hand so tightly into my chest that my arm begins to beat with my heart. I say to her out loud, "I know. I know. It's okay. I know. Just go have fun with them, okay? Don't cry. Stop crying. Be there with them all. I'll step aside tonight."

I wasn't happy when I first moved to this house. I was 20 minutes away from my old school, my old neighborhood, and I wasn't ready to leave. My parents did what was best for us by moving us away but I wasn't ready to leave and I was yanked out of our old home and placed in this new home and no one asked me for permission. No one asked me what I thought. No one asked me how it felt to leave a place that has felt like home and that maybe wasn't the safest but still somehow always protected you. No one asked.

On this drive home, I remember all of the late nights I rushed back to our house afraid my parents would still be awake when I got home past curfew. There is so much of me on these roads. On these sidewalks. The many many times I've walked before. The sadness in me spilling and staining the ground and even though I left, even though I tried to leave, I always come back here to this house.

Was I supposed to be asked if this is what I wanted? I remember watching a show about Siamese twins connected at the neck and there is always one, isn't there? One that wants to be freed from the other. And the other not feeling like they could survive alone. What if they could just stay together?

The anxiety and beating heart and the pulse racing and the pressure in your chest, the one you keep thinking is a heart attack, is me reminding you that I am here. It's me fighting for my life. Asking you, where am I supposed to go when you're here? These lights are on but they only flicker. When you start testosterone, will the black of patriarchy turn off all of these lights one by one? Will messy apologies sometimes bring them back on? Will you give me flowers but spit in their water as they try and grow?

I have never been happy. Being here, in this home, in San Diego, I've never been happy. I always felt empty and paranoid and afraid and loneliness is a mirror that pretends it's a window and I keep looking out of it thinking this is all there is to life, isn't it? I never got a chance to be happy. I never got a chance to feel beautiful.

And now, even with this anxiety you feel. How you feel maybe there is just something wrong with you. Maybe you are mentally unstable. That is me you are feeling. I am lost, too, my love. I am looking for me, too, my love.

I am lost.

I am lost.

I am lost.

I WILL MISS YOU, TOO

My nephew, Noah, is jumping up and down on the bed from excitement. "Auntie! Auntie! Auntie! I want to watch Super Monsters. I'm Frankie and you're Spike. Uncle Sean is Lobo."

"Noah, what if you start calling me Uncle Jae?"

"Noooo," he says, laughing. "I don't want you to be Uncle…you're my Auntie. And you're a boy."

When the night begins to end, I walk my sister and two nephews to the car. I wave goodbye to them both in their car seats and I smile. "You're my best friend!" I say to Noah. Little Jeremiah looks at me and smiles. I turn to my sister to say goodbye and she hugs me tight…and for a long time.

I feel her say, "I am going to miss you, sister" and she leaves without looking at me one more time.

She's never hugged us like that before. Will she know that I will miss her, too?

HER FINAL GOODBYE

I am packing the last items in my bag and I tell her, "I'm going to bring these suitcases downstairs now." I leave her in our bedroom.

This is an odd feeling. This room. How I have felt both safe and unsafe in it all at the same time. To know I will never come back here fully as I am right now. How do you begin to say goodbye? How will I be when I come back?

On the drive to the airport, I turn to my dad who is in the front seat and I say, "Remember I'm starting hormone therapy next week."

My dad pauses for only a second and then says, "Oh yeah? And you did all the research and everything?"

"Yep. I've talked to my doctors. Might even make my migraines go away since it can be related to estrogen."

He doesn't say anything. I change the topic.

When we get to the airport, I step away into the shadows.

I look at mom and dad and I hug them tight. "I will see you soon," I say.

I'm struggling today. I know I am giving myself
expectations of how I'm supposed to feel or act or what
to expect for tomorrow. I guess I thought I would be
much more excited than this. I guess maybe I am excited
but I'm also really scared. It's hard feeling so much grief
around me. My family and friends all experiencing a
sense of loss as I transition – and all of them have a right
to experience this the way they would. It's just... I
always have all of the answers, you know? I'm the fixer.
I'm the person they go to with the grief. And so what
am I supposed to do with that grief if my ultimate
happiness is the cause of it?

I have to remember that as long as I am accepting of
who I am, as I am in this exact moment, then I will
always be okay.

I have to give myself the permission to say out loud that
this is my body. And I have a right to my own
happiness. I do. I don't know how I will feel tomorrow
after getting the shot. I don't know if this fear is much
bigger than me again. I just have to yield.

To all the gods willing to listen to me right now...

I have found spirituality as I have grown to honor the
woman inside of me. I'm seeking help now. I am seeking
the strength and courage to be unapologetically me.
Nearly 3 years ago when I realized that I am a trans man,
I had no idea what this could look like. Now that I am
here, one day before my first T shot, I can't believe what
I have overcome to have this exact moment. It must
mean that there is something bigger. I don't know how
I—as just human—could have done this without some

divine intervention. I need strength. I need light as I
retreat into the darkness.

I want to be excited. I want this to feel right all the time.
I want to no longer be terrified. I want to be me. I want
to feel like me.

To all the gods willing to listen to me right now...I feel
the weakest I have ever been. I surrender to you now.
Tell me that everything is going to be okay. Tell me the
grief around me will settle with the dust and the only
thing left from all of this mess is me with so much man
and woman and an entire swallowed spectrum of gender
just unapologetically existing. I am on my knees
surrendering. I know I can't do this alone.

DAY 1 OF T

Are you ready?

I'm sitting on the metro heading to the clinic and I jump back a little hearing her voice.

"I didn't think you'd be here."

God, good thing you're going through this transition because you actually are a dumb dude. Why wouldn't I be here?

"What do I always say?! Men are trash but I'm like...recyclable trash. Still trash but you know...less."

Um. Okay. That was a trashy thing to say.

"I didn't think you'd be here because I know you're afraid that as I start taking T shots, you'll disappear more and more."

Will I?

"No, I don't think so - I hope not. I want you to stay. I want this to be our life together. I want us both happy."

Grandma came to us last night in a dream. I'm not sure if you remember. She wants to tell you that you don't feel excitement about today because you just upped your anti-depressant dose for your migraines. Your system is a little out of whack right now trying to get used to that. Adding testosterone to the mix might make it a little more challenging. You should know that doesn't mean it's not the right thing for you. She also told me that when your physical body feels like it's failing you, then those are the times you should feel me most inside of you. To remind you that you are okay. You will be okay.

You will be okay today after your shot.

I will be okay today after my shot.

DAY 14 OF T

My love,

I have been growing harder. I can feel the already small parts of me that were soft thickening and molding itself into something tougher than even I could have created.

I have been on testosterone for 14 days. On days 1-3 of the injections, I have so much energy that I am not sure where to place it. Something tells me I should place that energy within myself as a spiritual investment. Perhaps, that "something" is you.

If you were to ask me 15 days ago what would happen to the woman inside of me as I started taking T, I might've answered that I would feel you disappearing. Angry, maybe. Resentful. Alone. Hurt. But...I don't feel that - I haven't felt that. You're still here. For the most part, you give me my space and stand back but other times, like tonight, you are right beside me. The inner voice reminding me that from this place of centeredness you helped me feel tonight, that is where I can make decisions. That is where I will learn how to be happy.

I have been struggling with the fact that it has been two weeks and I am still unhappy. I think maybe you got yourself to a better place before my first T shot than I did. I was so focused on the end result that I didn't stop to appreciate my journey. And now I am here. Wondering how I got to this place at 1:30am on Day 14 and I have just ended a year long relationship with the first woman I let experience me as this man I am learning how to become.

It was difficult to end things - especially because of my fear that I will always be alone without anyone who will truly fight to understand me. I'm scared I won't ever trust another person again. I'm scared I won't experience the type of love that redefines me. She loved me in a way that was just beginning. And after a year, after so much time, I knew that if I didn't end things to give myself this space, I would refuse to acknowledge that a love that is just beginning will only keep us at the starting line. I'm too competitive to not fight for a love that will bring us both in the lead - even if it means separating so we can get a head start. And I loved her too much to just keep our engines revving.

Is it wrong—or maybe weird—that now my standard is to find a woman who reminds me so much of you? Isn't that ironic? These past 3 years of myself as a shadow man in contention with you—a woman, a Queen in her actual right, and a true force—yet now that I am turning biologically male, I am now looking for you in the women I speak to or spend my time with. I'm looking for something familiar. A laugh shared, a late night full of stories, maybe some karaoke, a first date full of too much transparency. Something. How is it that you are right beside me tonight but I am still so desperate to look for you?

Does this mean I am learning to truly love myself? Is this what this new depression is? The feeling of loss around me to make space for gaining self-love? Have I just not had the space to hold this love in? Is this why I felt so strongly about ending things with a woman who would love me to her grave? Because I realized I needed to make space for this new self-love? Interesting. I hope it's true. Self-love has been a bedtime story I've been telling myself for too many years. I go to sleep eager to dream up visions of how good my life could be if I were happy. If I just loved what I saw in the mirror. If I could just love myself wholly as I am and as I turn into what I am supposed to be. I don't have too many good dreams. Maybe because I needed to make the space to have them.

Moon Goddess says I have been too stubborn to listen. She is right. I am as stubborn as they come. The Aries ram could not be more correct for my spirit's character. Tonight, I learned about Cernunnos, Lord of Wild Things, sometimes symbolic of a rebirth. Is this darkness I am feeling death? Death of old habits and patterns and self-loathing? Am I experiencing another awakening? The images of Cernunnos with a crescent moon is symbolic of union with female energies. Isn't all of this what you and I are trying to do now?

As I learned on, I found His connection to the Moon. Once again, I am reminded of how arrogant I am to think just because I could not hear Her throughout all this, it meant She abandoned me. Of course - I'm such a fucking idiot. Only you can hear Her. It is my union with your feminine energy that is allowing me to listen again. She did not abandon us. We are all here together. And tonight, I feel multiple gods surrounding me as I write this letter to you as a form of prayer.

Maybe tonight, as I have freed some space inside of me, I can experience a new awakening as a man. Just as you did all those years ago. Maybe this was supposed to be our timeline in this life. Maybe we both had to suffer individually before finally accepting we need each other in order to feel whole.

I love you. Thank you for being with me tonight. Thank you for not leaving when you were within your right (and most would argue you should've). You're still here. I am still here. We are still here.

DAY 16 OF T

Can you help take this sadness away? Was the
testosterone supposed to make all of this better? Am I
supposed to feel better? Why is this so painful? My
dysphoria is the Earth's shadow and I am the sun stuck
in a lunar eclipse. Wondering: when will they see me
shine again?

THE SOUND OF GRIEF

The grief became too heavy tonight. As I sobbed, a noise came out of me that I have never heard before. Is this what my grief sounds like? A woman wailing? Is this me? Is this her? I let it happen. Grief wrapped its arms around me and it's funny how it oddly feels so safe. Like I can stay here.

Ordinary tasks have become extraordinary to complete. I just want to go somewhere safe. Even if that's somewhere in my head.

As I lie on the couch, I imagine I am resting my head on her lap as I sob. She is sobbing, too. But there is comfort here. Amongst all of this pain - a pain we cannot name - there is still some peace. I feel that now. After I have sobbed and heard the grief leave my body through my mouth. It's peaceful now.

How long do we stay here?

I have never been extraordinary. Though people have told me that many times before. We feel like a leaky faucet. We have to get up. We can't stay here. The darkness has a way of tricking you into thinking it will keep you safe if you just can't open your eyes to see the wreckage in front of you.

But open your eyes, my love. We have to open our eyes. We have to find the light again.

BACK TO THE START

How do I begin to start knowing who I am? Maybe a
part of me always thought that there is nothing else to
evolve into. I feel reborn. I feel like an infant born into
this world. I am relearning how to walk, fall, then get up
again. The dangers to avoid. Who to trust. Who I can
make laugh. Who will love me when I figure this all out?
Will I be as charming as her? Will I have the same
confidence as her? Or will I crumble? Am I weak. Am I
strong. Who am I. Who is this man. Tonight, I did not
feel like a man while sitting in the back of a car with
white cis men at the front. I thought: how do I connect
here as a trans man—as a brown trans man—where do I
connect? Where can I go that feels like home? Where
can I go? Where I can be seen by more than just me?
Because sometimes, I get tired of trying to look so damn
hard. Who will be there when I am on the other side?
What will the love be like? How will I be like? How will
I be?

She never got a chance to truly let someone in. Did she
ever want to? My love, did you want to?

*It took this. All this man in your spirit and in those syringes. It
took this for me to realize it is actually all I ever wanted. To not
teach someone how to love me. To just show up and be loved in all
of the pieces I have picked up from behind. All I ever wanted was
for someone to be brave enough to stick around. To fight. The way
I know I could've. I am tired now. Just as you are, my love. We
are hungry for more. Our appetite is finally bigger than the
mediocrity. We want excellence. It is sad here, yes. Where we are.
It is lonely and the night is full of reminders of other places we
could be. But we are here together. In this lonely Boston hotel
room. Lying on this king bed in silence. It is just us here. We can
love just us here. It will come, my love. Our greatest love...they will
come.*

MENSTRUATING WHILE ON T

You're a loser

You're a winner

Fuck you

Go away

Come closer

Why aren't you fighting to come closer

WHY ARE YOU SO GOD DAMN CLOSE YOU'RE
SMOTHERING ME

Wait, don't go

I miss my nephews omg what if they forget who I am

What if I forget who I am

Why did they "she" me what did I do wrong

IT'S "HE/HIM" FUCKWAD

I'm sad

I'm lonely

I'm so smart

This is so fucking dumb

I want to quit

I'm tired of white people hurting me

I want to throw a fucking plate against the wall

What are you, a fucking victim? Quit complaining.

I want pizza.

You can't have gluten.

I want pizza.

You also can't have dairy.

I CAN'T HAVE ANYTHING.

You're being dramatic.

I'M SO FUCKING LIMITED.

You're still being dramatic.

Who the fuck is going to love me?

Do I have lupus? I have a rash. Is this lupus?

I have acne.

You don't have acne.

I HAVE ACNE WHAT IS THIS.

It's not a pimple.

Oh.

I'm fat.

I hate my boobs.

I'm never going to get the body I want.

Holy shit, look how broad my shoulders are.

WHY DO I KEEP BLEEDING

WHY DO I KEEP BLEEDING

Sup, bro

I want ice cream.

Yeah…you still can't have dairy.

FUCK.

HELLO?

"'Hello?' That's not even a real title."

Shut up.

"You shut up."

You've been ignoring me.

"You've been ignoring me."

Jesus, WILL YOU STOP?

"Nope."

You've been ignoring me.

"You've been annoying me."

I haven't even been around for me to annoy you.

"Well. You're around now, aren't you?"

What's your problem?

"You. You're my fucking problem."

"I hate you today. Today, you are not my greatest love. You are not even my decent love. Today, I wish you never existed. Today, I wish I was born with a penis and not a vagina. Today, I hate you so much. I just. I hate you. I HATE YOU.

Why is this my body? This flimsy looking body that looks like no one tries to take care of it. I try so hard for my body. I try so hard for everyone. I have no more forgiveness.

The amount of *she* I have been hearing is turning itself into bricks and being shoved down my throat. Why don't they understand that being called *she* sometimes feels like a death threat?

I'm so tired. I'm so tired of hating you. I'm tired of trying to find love here. I'm tired of trying to keep all of the god damn lights on in here. Today, it is so dark that I can actually see what's in front of me. Nothing.

Today, I am nothing. Just a flimsy body. With no appeal. Today, I looked in the mirror and saw a monster. It laughs at me. Every day, the monster laughs at me.

Where can I go for love? Where can I go where no one wants forgiveness or explanations from me anymore? Where can I go?

Today is the first day I truly hated my boobs. TRULY. I imagine them gone. I imagine what my chest would look like. I ask if I will ever go swimming again. Will I ever swim shirtless and full of love for myself?"

Or will you always wear the layers to hide? Will you always say you don't want to feel the water today? But you do. You want to feel the water, my love. You wish for the salt to cascade into an avalanche over your body. You wish to feel seasoned in this body.

"Who am I? Who is this talking? Where did you come from? The dark place? I didn't think there could be another one of you down there. I thought I got rid of you all. But I didn't, did I?

Today. I hate myself. Today, I still don't want to die but kind of purse my lips to also say, 'Well. Sometimes, though.'

Is that true? What is this self-hate manifesting itself into gym time and Rubik's time and time blurring itself into a machine that stays on even when the power is off? This hate that has me sitting here writing it out of me as if to say, to prove on paper, 'HEY I AM HERE.' I met you today, Hate. I want to die today. And I am relieved I can finally admit that."

You don't mean that. YOU CAN'T LIE, REMEMBER? This isn't death. This is a bad day. This is the 8th bad day in a row. That's what this is.

My love. You have been ignoring me. You've been refusing to hear me whisper to you when you are lonely.

"THEY KEEP CALLING FOR YOU, JERRICA. FOR YOU. FOR JERRICA, SHE IS GREAT. FOR JERRICA, SHE IS AMAZING. FOR JERRICA – SHE SHE SHE SHE. THEY KEEP FUCKING CALLING FOR YOU. NO ONE IS CALLING FOR ME.

No one is fucking calling. For. Me.

I want someone to call for me and believe it's me. I want to be seen whole, not half a man or half a woman or even a whole self that is non-binary. I want someone to see me because most days, I have to use every strength in my bones to even see myself. They keep calling for you. I keep trying to answer for you to remind them it's me. It's me here. She's not here. Don't call for her. Then when I answer for you they say that it doesn't make sense. Or that it will take time. Or that they'll get there. Or that they're still getting used to it. Or that they're so sorry. Or that they will be better next time. OR they mean they mean they mean they mean. THEY MEAN. THEY MEAN. THEY MEAN. SORRY, I MEANT HE.

That's what they all say to me when they call for you and I try to answer, instead.

How can I love and hate you this much all together? How. I've been ignoring you because everyone else is not ignoring you. Everyone else misses you. They miss you.

No one misses me. Not even the woman who says she loves me. Even she doesn't miss ME. She misses parts of you. You. I know. Because she called me pretty the other night. I know that's why.

Forgive them all, they say. You have to. It is the only way to not get here. Anymore. You have to forgive them and everything they mean."

I can't. You're not letting me surface, my love. I keep trying. I know you feel me. I know you feel the tears behind your eyes. I'm trying to come for you. I'm trying to call for you. You're not letting me surface. You have to let me surface. It is the only way I can show you the light out of here. Jae.

Maybe your name is not Jae. Maybe that name still feels like me. You need to change your name. Maybe you need to change your name. I can't help you if you don't let me come for you. I can't prove to you that I see you if you refuse to even look at me. If you don't let me out of your eyes. Let me show you how to get out, my love. Let me call for you.

Let me call for you.

THE FORMULA FOR FORGIVENESS

If I am *she* 34 times in a day
And I am only he twice
What is the difference between me and *her*?
How do we add up?

If 34 times in a day
Multiplies by 2
Each time a *she*
Takes me by the neck
What is the product of my identity?

For every:

Old habits die hard
We'll get there
It's going to take everyone some time
That's not what I meant
It'll take some getting used to
You have to be a little more understanding
Just be patient with us
It's hard to remember

For every:

Hey, just a reminder my pronouns are he/him
Hi, can someone chat her to let her know what my
pronouns are?
Hello, I would appreciate it if you would use my
pronouns
Just a reminder my pronouns are he/him
You didn't use my pronouns at all today

For every: -

I mean he

I'm sorry, I meant he
His pronouns are he/him
You mean he
His, not *hers*
Remember he
It's he/him

That has not been said
On my behalf
From my family
And friends

For every:

She – with no follow-up
With no correction
With no apology
Just *she*
Just this bomb
Just the salt into the wound I've learned how to disguise
Into a chuckle
Into a smile
Into
I forgive you
Once again

I forgive you all
Once again

I will solve this problem for you all
Once again

Don't worry about the math
Once again

I will solve this on my own

Once again.

MY MOURNING ROUTINE

1. Wake up
2. Run hand over stomach – is there a 6-pack yet? No?
3. Sigh
4. Get up
5. Look in mirror
6. Sigh
7. Stare at mirror
8. Stare at mirror
9. Brush teeth
10. Floss
11. Take off shirt
12. Stare at mirror
13. Take off bottoms
14. Stare at mirror
15. Stare at mirror
16. Step in shower
17. Shampoo
18. Conditioner
19. Body wash
20. Wash parts
21. Stare at parts
22. Hold parts
23. Sigh
24. Get out of shower
25. Dry myself with a towel
26. Stand in front of the mirror naked
27. Stare at mirror
28. Stare at mirror
29. Stare at mirror
30. Stare at mirror
31. Stare at mirror
32. Stare at mirror
33. Put arms up laterally
34. Look at biceps. Think: Have you grown yet?

35. Stare at mid-section in the mirror
36. Stare at mirror
37. Stare at mirror
38. Turn to side
39. Stare at mirror
40. Sigh
41. Put lotion on
42. Put on underwear
43. Put on tight sports bra
44. Struggle to put on tight sports bra
45. Put on under shirt
46. Stare at mirror
47. Put on clothes for the day
48. Stare at mirror
49. Change top
50. Stare at mirror
51. Change back to original top
52. Stare at mirror
53. Change to a third top
54. Stare at mirror
55. Sigh
56. Grab sweater
57. Grab layers
58. Hide body
59. Stare at mirror
60. Sigh
61. Look at time – I'm late, again.
62. Stare at mirror
63. Hold back tears
64. Walk out door.

MY LAST PERIOD

I knew.

The same way you know when a relationship is about to
end.

Like a goodbye
That only one side is ready to say
When the other side just wants to keep saying

Hello, again.
Hello

I am the mark of woman

And I should be here.

I CAN BARELY HEAR YOU

"The weirdest thing just happened. I was in the shower just now and tried to sing Adele's, 'Crazy for You,' and when I tried to falsetto, I COULDN'T DO IT. Nothing came out. Maybe I'm getting sick or something."

No.

"No, what?"

No. You're not getting sick.

"I can barely hear you."

I said you're not getting sick.

"Wait. Why are you crying?"

Nothing.

"What? Why are you whispering?"

I SAID. NOTHING.

"Hey, look at me. It's clearly something. Why are you so upset?"

You're not getting sick. And I'm not whispering. Your voice is dropping.

"Oh. And I can barely hear you because..."

...because my voice is disappearing.

"Wait, no. That's not how this is supposed to work. Your voice isn't supposed to disappear just because mine is dropping. How do we stop this?"

We can't.

"I think we can! Maybe we can start doing voice exercises together in the morning. And we'll end our nights with like...I don't know ginger lemon tea or something. We'll get our voices stronger together."

Jae. It doesn't work like that. I know you want to keep us together. But I'm disappearing. I don't bleed every month anymore—my cycle is gone. Your testosterone levels became mine and I can't conceive this way. You've started the inquiry about top surgery. Your face is getting wider, more square. The soft parts of me are getting weighed down by muscle forming. And now I'm the god damn Little Mermaid losing my voice for a man. I knew I always hated Disney.

"I don't know what to say."

Well. Learn what to say. Because soon, you will be the only one between us who will have the ability to say anything.

"I want us to stay together. I don't think we have to approach this as you going away so I can be here. That's not what I want."

Then what do you want? You can still stop this. If you get off testosterone now, your voice will stop dropping and I can stay here with you.

"But...I don't want to stop taking testosterone. I mean yeah my dysphoria is through the fucking roof. I hate what I see in the mirror. I feel hefty. Big. Swollen. Ugly. I'm lonely. I'm full of grief. But...there is also moments of joy here. And I know it will get better. I don't want to stop. And I don't want you to disappear, either."

You can't have both.

"I think I can."

You can't.

"We can. Jerrica, I think we can.

Jerrica?

JERRICA. WE CAN."

THE DAY SHE BECOMES A MORTICIAN

When they wheel my body in front of her
She will ask for some privacy

My body will be cold in her hands
She will begin to cry.

The fluorescent lighting in the room will show the
stubble under my chin
That I did not shave the morning I died

"Are you ready?" she will say
She will wait for my response
As she has done for decades

When she sprays my body with disinfectant
She will remember back on the conversation we had
about when and how I would die
"I would hope that I would go expectedly.
Not from a peanut, god no. Not from a peanut.
I didn't live my entire life fighting to be exactly who I
am for a peanut to take me out.
No...not that way.
I hope not from a car accident like our mother's psychic
predicted.
Not from cancer or illness...though these days, it's hard
to imagine it won't be that.
I don't know
I guess I'm afraid of dying alone while walking on the
street
With strangers watching and murmuring about my slow
escape from Earth."
She will remember the story I told her about the time I
got off the metro
And walked up the stairs in the station only to see a
woman lying on the floor near the elevator

Lifeless
Paramedics at her side administering CPR
And the way that I could not take my eyes off of her
hands
How with every pump the paramedic made on her chest
Her hands would move but only to go back to remaining
lifeless each time the paramedic stopped
She will remember how hard that was for me
How I silently wished the woman on the floor would
never be me
That I hoped the woman had family who would wonder
about where she was in a couple of hours
That someone who was kind was nearby
She will remember how she told me, "Maybe she didn't
die. Maybe she turned out to be okay."
But how she also felt me inside knowing it wasn't true.

She will go back to the stubble under my chin
Count the hair on my chest
And begin to shave me
She will jokingly hear me say, "HEY I worked hard to
grow that!"
And she will laugh out loud
As if I was right there next to her

Then she will place her hands on my chest
My scars looking more alive than me
She will run her fingers to my shoulders
And then to the sides of my neck
She will remember the years of chronic pain
And headaches
The cost of hiding a body naturally given
For the benefit of truly being seen
She will start to apply pressure with her fingertips
To break the rigor mortis
Behind her
She can almost hear me letting out a sigh of relief

This last time my body will feel so tense from hiding

She will then move her fingers to my eyelids
And she will pause
She knows this is one of the most important parts:
setting my eyes
She grabs a small piece of cotton and places it between
my lid and eye to round it off
She will remember the times I stared in the mirror and
yelled,
"WE NEED TO PUT TEA BAGS UNDER OUR
EYES. WE'RE LOOKING OLD."
She will laugh again and pierce the silence with her
nostalgia
A part of her will want to make my eyes ridiculously
round and huge
Just to make me angry one last time

Then, she will move her hands to my mouth
And gently place a mouth form to hold my jaw together
"I keep having dreams of me losing teeth easily. It
terrifies me," I used to tell her in the mornings
She will remember the braces she wore
And the day they finally came off
She will remember looking in the mirror and thinking
she looked like a beaver
But how I took such good care of our teeth later on
after a dentist scared me into flossing everyday
Until my final days
She will outline my jaw with her fingertips
And remember all of the times I wished mine was more
defined
She will try to set the jawline as I wished it always could
be

And then she will moisturize my features
Remembering the eczema

The gallons and gallons of lotion used in our lifetime to
resemble skin that was somewhat normal

This next part is harder for her to start
The part where she chooses the incision site to embalm
my arteries
While simultaneously draining the blood from my heart
She will look down at my left wrist
And remember the nights she made her own incisions
How she was sobbing each time then automatically
stopped crying the second she saw the blood
How here, in this moment
She has permission to make a final incision
The same final incision that had crossed her mind every
now and again
She will remember how I, too, looked at the scars every
morning
How I liked to remember
How I missed it the same way she did
How sometimes we wanted more

She will let out a sigh
And realize she had stopped crying this entire time

She will make the incision
And watch as her hands are the steadiest they have ever
been
When she turns on the embalming machine to distribute
the fluid
While simultaneously watching my blood, my mark of
life, leaving my body
And replacing it with formaldehyde-based chemical
solutions
To delay my decomposition
She will remember the time I came home from work
one day after filming inside of a cadaver lab for 10 hours

Saying, "Ugh, I could not unsmell the formaldehyde. I
smelled it in my lunch. On me. Everywhere."
She will remember how we laughed about it
How it wasn't eerie, when most would have thought it
should be
"Not us," she will think
"We do not scare easily."
We know how scary actual life can be
A fight to have autonomy over your own self
To say "love" to yourself
To mean it
She will remember us laughing
Until the smell of the chemicals snaps her out of the
memory
Until she is alone in the dark room again
With my body lit under the fluorescents

And after she has embalmed my cavity
And cleaned the insides of my organs
She knows the next step is the most delicate step of
them all:

The washing of my body one last time.

She will take disinfectant and begin to wipe me down
She will start crying again at this point
And she will find that she has to wipe her tears away
from the spots she has already cleaned
But on my chest
A pool of tears will remain
"Take me with you"
She will say
Her tears will be the holy water that will be buried with
me

And when she dresses my body in a suit specifically
tailored for me

And for this occasion
She will remember all of the times we went to a tailor
together
The many times the men looked at us confused
And the women tailors they sent in, instead, who wanted
to accentuate the hips I always tried to hide
The many times we told them, "No. Straight down."
The many times we got our suits back and it fit in the
obvious way
But never in the way I would have liked

This time
My suit will fit me perfectly
She will tie my tie in the fast, remedial way that we
always joked was good enough to get the job done
A tie clip
A pocket square

And then she will move to my hair
Out of her purse, she will take out the two pomades I
have used for decades
The first to use before blow drying, and then again in
the middle of blow drying
And the second pomade to finish
She will have made sure that my haircut was done right

And when she is all done
When I am lying on the mortuary table
Looking the most man I have ever been
And with every hair strand in place
She will step back and say,

"What a beauty you are, my love.
What a beauty you are."

And she will step further into the darkness
Until she is gone

Just like me
Her last grand gesture of love toward me
As a way to take a part of her with me to the other side

And I will have known
In my last dying days
That I didn't tell her enough how she was not just the
woman inside of me
But the spirit inside of me
That the times I couldn't find god
She was the closest I could feel to a miracle
And that when I died
It would be the day she is finally free of me
Free to be the woman I shamed her into being
Too many times to count in this lifetime

Her last grand gesture of love toward me
Will be a testament of her sacrifice all of these years
Of being, yet again, another woman pushed into the
shadows
So that the man can step into the light
How the feminist in me will always be sorry of this
But never sorry enough to keep myself in the dark

The woman inside of me
My dear, sweet woman inside of me
The woman I have hated and loved
She has to be the one to prepare my body when I die…

She is the only one who has ever truly known how.

EPILOGUE

Dear Little One,

Our sweet boy. They will be cruel to you. When you try to put on the clothes that are too big for your slender body, the other boys on your street will laugh at you. When you walk by them in school, they will yell, "LOOK AT THAT UGLY GIRL!! SHE'S SO UGLY. YOU'RE NOT A BOY!!!" They will throw things at you when you walk by. You will hear over and over again: You're ugly. You're ugly. You're ugly.

When you take up skateboarding as a passion, those same boys will ring your doorbell and ask you to come to the door. When you do, you will hope they are finally asking you to play outside with them. Instead, the leader of the group will say, "We keep hearing you trying to do tricks with your skateboard. You're such a poser." Then they will laugh and run away. The next week, you will be on your skateboard in front of your house. The boys will come by and tell you to do a kickflip. You will tell them to go away. They will say, "Do a kickflip or you're a poser." You will do a kickflip but not land it. They will laugh some more. When you walk by them in school, they will yell, "POSER!!! POSER!!!!" You will second guess buying skater clothes and shoes – afraid the boys will torment you more. Afraid they will beat you up and take your things. Afraid the clothes for boys will sink the truth in your skin: You're ugly. You're ugly. You're ugly.

In the 7th grade, you're going to cut your hair short. The boys will laugh when you walk into the classroom. They will say, "SHE'S REALLY TRYING TO BE A BOY! UGLY POSER!!" You will look in the mirror at your short hair. A part of you will recognize yourself while the other part of you will whisper: Am I ugly? Am I ugly? Am I ugly?

So you will slowly begin to wear dresses. And short skirts. Those same boys who gave you so much fear to walk outside of your home will find you again in high school. This time, the leader will come up to you at a party. He will call you "darling." He will say you're beautiful. He will ask you to give him a chance. You will tell him, "You made my life miserable when we were kids." He will say, "I was a stupid kid. C'mon, you can forgive me."
You'll go on a few dates. But as you are out together, as he continues to call you "darling," all you will hear is: You're ugly. You're ugly. You're ugly.

Little one, our sweet boy. You are not ugly.

You are strong.

You are brave.

You are beautiful.

You are gorgeous.

You are handsome.

You are stunning.

Those boys in the neighborhood. Those boys at school who never gave you attention until you started showing them some skin. You will never be like them. That is not the man you will become.

You will be a man that shows strength in your tenderness. You will not swallow your feelings and tears thinking it makes you more man. You will embrace all of your parts. You will love the people in your life so fiercely, so relentlessly, they will wonder who

*taught you how. And it will be you. You taught yourself how to
love others because of what it took to finally try to love yourself.*

You will never give up on yourself. Even if it seems
easier. Even if you wish you could. You will show
everyone, once again, what it looks like to stand back up.
We are so proud of you, little one. You are loved. You
are not ugly. You are beautiful.

You are beautiful. You are beautiful. You are beautiful.

Made in the USA
Las Vegas, NV
15 August 2022